IMPORTANT JOBS

AT AIRPORTS

by Mari Bolte

PEBBLE
a capstone imprint

Published by Pebble Explore, an imprint of Capstone
1710 Roe Crest Drive, North Mankato, Minnesota 56003
capstonepub.com

Library of Congress Cataloging-in-Publication Data is available on the Library of Congress website.

ISBN 9780756572082 (hardcover)
ISBN 9780756572037 (paperback)
ISBN 9780756572044 (ebook PDF)

Summary: Gives readers basic info about often and less often-considered jobs at airports.

Image Credits
Alamy: Agencja Fotograficzna Caro, 23; Getty Images: Digital Vision, 6, Fuse, 9, gorodenkoff, 10, RgStudio, 14, uuoott, 24, wundervisuals, 21; Newscom/BSIP, 18; Shutterstock: 06photo, 28, Anirut Thailand, 17, Corepics VOF, 27, Real_life_photo, 13, tong patong, Cover (bottom), Tyler Olson, Cover (top), William Perugini, 5

Editorial Credits
Editor: Mandy R. Robbins; Designer: Dina Her; Media Researcher: Jo Miller; Production Specialist: Tori Abraham

All internet sites appearing in back matter were available and accurate when this book was sent to press.

Printed and bound in China. PO5132

TABLE OF CONTENTS

Words in **bold** are in the glossary.

FLY THE FRIENDLY SKIES

Airplanes fly high! They take people all over the world. Airplanes land and take off at airports. The world has around 41,000 airports. But these places don't run themselves! Many people work at airports. Find out what they do. Every job is important!

> **FACT**
> The United States has around 13,500 airports.

PILOTS

Without a pilot, a plane can't fly! Pilots control the airplane. They are in charge of keeping everyone on the airplane safe. They check the weather before takeoff. Storms, ice, and wind makes flying harder.

A pilot plans the best way to go. Pilots talk to air traffic control and ground crews. They make sure it is safe to take off and land the plane.

SECURITY

Security workers keep people safe. If they see a **threat**, they deal with it quietly. They do not want to scare other travelers. Special machines look inside **luggage**. They help spot dangerous items. Security workers also make sure no one is carrying weapons.

Air marshals are security in the sky. They fly on planes with passengers. These workers try not to stand out. They wear normal clothes. If something dangerous happens, they step in to help.

AIR TRAFFIC CONTROLLERS

There are no traffic lights in the sky! Air traffic controllers tell pilots when to take off and land. They keep track of every plane. Without these workers, planes might run into each other.

If a pilot needs help landing, air traffic controllers are there! Controllers must be smart. They must speak clearly and stay calm under pressure.

BAGGAGE HANDLERS

Some passengers carry what they need in a bag. Others use larger luggage. Large bags and suitcases are piled together.

Baggage handlers place luggage in a special area under the plane. They make sure to store it on the right plane. When a plane lands, handlers take bags off the plane.

They put them on a **conveyer belt**. Then passengers find them. Baggage handlers are strong. They lift heavy bags. They treat them with care.

MECHANICS

Airplanes are fast. They fly far. They must be cared for. Mechanics keep planes from breaking down. They keep everyone safe.

Mechanics look for wear and tear. Wheels must turn and stop properly. Doors must stay closed tightly and open when needed. Electronics must be checked. If something is broken, mechanics fix it.

FACT

Large airports in big cities are called hubs.

GIFT SHOP EMPLOYEES

Are you hungry or thirsty? Did you forget something? Are you looking for a game to play while you wait? Do you want a book to read during your trip? Airport gift shop employees can help! You can find snacks, books, magazines and more at gift shops.

Sometimes, visitors want to remember where they have been. Gift shops sell postcards, key chains, and other local items.

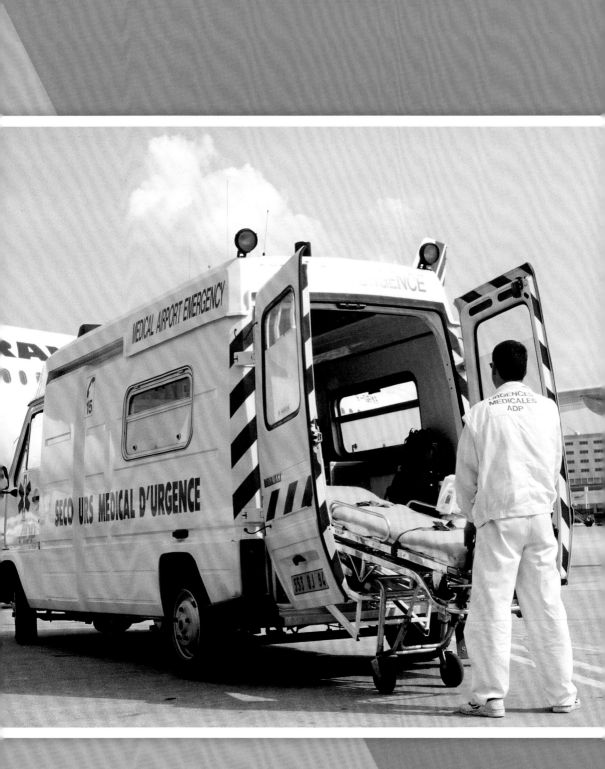

MEDICAL OFFICERS

Health problems can happen anywhere. A person may get hurt or sick at the airport. Medical officers help quickly. They give people emergency care. They decide if a person needs to go to a hospital.

Planes make emergency landings if a passenger is ill. Medical officers are ready when they land. A sick person might be **contagious**. Then medical officers check everyone on the flight. They also make sure pilots and flight crew are fit for duty.

CHECK-IN OFFICERS

Check-in officers tell people when their plane is ready. Is the plane running late? These workers let everyone know.

Passengers must have a ticket to fly. The name on the ticket must match the passenger's **ID**. Check-in officers make sure the person has the right ticket. They check carry-on bags. If a bag is too big, the officer takes it. It gets stored with the other large luggage.

CUSTODIANS

Many people pass through airports. They eat. They drink. They take naps and use the restroom. Passengers may be there for hours. Then they get on their plane and leave. Sometimes they leave a mess behind. Custodians pick it up. They clean carpets. They empty trash cans and tidy parking lots. They keep airports neat and clean.

> **FACT**
> The Dallas-Fort Worth airport made 32,000 tons of solid waste in 2021. Most of it was from food.

FLIGHT ATTENDANTS

You step onto an airplane. A flight attendant greets you. Do you need help with your bag? They can help.

The safety and comfort of passengers is a flight attendant's **responsibility**. If there is a problem on board, the flight attendant will take charge. If there is an emergency, flight attendants show passengers what to do.

SHUTTLE DRIVERS

Many people need rides to the airport. **Shuttle** drivers pick up passengers. They take them where they need to go. Sometimes, people need to get across a big airport fast. Other times, they need a ride to their hotel. They may need a lift back to their own car. Shuttle drivers make sure people get to the right place.

> ### FACT
> Almost every airport has a three-letter code. This code makes it easy to identify the airport's location. Airlines have two-letter codes.

Airports are busy places. Airport workers make sure passengers get where they need to go. They keep passengers safe and comfortable. They help people with medical needs. These jobs are all important. Would you want to work at an airport? What job would you do?

OTHER JOBS AT THE AIRPORT

Immigration Officers

People who travel overseas need special books called passports. **Immigration** officers make sure visitors have permission to be in that country.

Caterers

Some flights are long. People need to eat! Caterers prepare meals that can easily be eaten on an airplane. They make sure meals are delivered fresh and on time.

Aircraft Fuelers

Airplanes need fuel to fly. It is important they have just the right amount to get to their next stop. Aircraft fuelers keep track of that amount and make sure planes are fueled correctly.

GLOSSARY

contagious (kun-TAY-juss)—spreadable, as in a disease

conveyer belt (kuhn-VAY-uhr BELT)—a moving belt that carries objects from one place to another

ID (eye-DEE)—something that proves who a person is

immigration (im-uh-GRAY-shun)—the act of moving to another country to live permanently

luggage (LUG-uhj)—baggage holding traveler's belongings; often a suitcase

responsibility (ri-spon-suh-BIL-uh-tee)—a duty or a job

shuttle (SHUT-uhl)—a vehicle used to transport people back and forth

threat (THRET)—a person or situation considered dangerous

READ MORE

Heuer, Lourdes. *On This Airplane*. Plattsburgh, NY: Tundra Books of Northern New York, 2022.

Rhodes, Sam. *STEAM Jobs for Gearheads*. North Mankato, MN: Capstone Press, 2019.

Rossiter, Brienna. *We Need Transportation Workers*. Lake Elmo, MN: Focus Readers, 2022.

INTERNET SITES

Behind the Scenes at the Airport
funkidslive.com/learn/behind-scenes-airport/people-see-airport/

Britannica for Kids: Airports
kids.britannica.com/students/article/airport/272760

Six Reasons the Airport is the Best Place to Work
aviationpros.com/ground-handling/ground-handlers-service-providers/blog/21242199/aviator-six-reasons-the-airport-is-the-best-place-to-work

INDEX

ABOUT THE AUTHOR

Mari Bolte is an author and editor of children's books on all sorts of subjects, from graphic novels about science to art projects to hands-on history. She lives in southern Minnesota in the middle of a forest full of animals.